For

TO HAVE
&
TO HOLD

A Celebration of Marriage

Edited by Lois L. Kaufman

Design by Lesley Ehlers
Photographs by Solomon M. Skolnick

PETER PAUPER PRESS, INC.
WHITE PLAINS, NEW YORK

For Bill

Pressed flower art by Tauna Andersen
courtesy of *Pressed for Time*, Ephraim, Utah

Wedding toasts by John P. Beilenson

Copyright © 1995
Peter Pauper Press, Inc.
202 Mamaroneck Avenue
White Plains, NY 10601
All rights reserved
ISBN 0-88088-884-9
Printed in Singapore
7 6 5 4 3 2 1

Contents

Introduction

To have and to hold from this day forward, for better for worse, for richer for poorer, in sickness and in health, to love and to cherish, till death us do part.

THE BOOK OF COMMON PRAYER

These words, or variations on them, have become familiar to all who have witnessed or taken part in marriage ceremonies over the years. Herein, each phrase of this solemnization is followed by a corresponding wedding toast and becomes a point of departure for relevant quotations.

We hope that this book will help you to celebrate the joyful day that brought you together.

L. L. K.

From This Day Forward

This wedding day is the first of marriage's many days. It is a joyful celebration, one that sets the tone for each day's smaller, but no less important, celebrations. So let us toast the bride and groom:

From this day forward,
May all your days be filled with celebrations,
Celebrations great and small,
Celebrations of love and happiness.

Come live with me, and be my love,
And we will some new pleasures prove
Of golden sands, and crystal brooks,
With silken lines, and silver hooks.

JOHN DONNE

A good marriage is one which allows for change
and growth in the individuals and in the way they
express their love.

PEARL S. BUCK

I think that when you have a great love, and
you're secure in that, it doesn't matter how far
apart you are.

JULIA ROBERTS

Marriage is a mistake of youth—which we should all make.

Marriage is the alliance of two people, one of whom never remembers birthdays and the other who never forgets them.

OGDEN NASH

Marriage must constantly fight against a monster which devours everything: routine.

HONORÉ DE BALZAC

An ideal wife is any woman who has an ideal husband.

BOOTH TARKINGTON

The best friend is likely to acquire the best wife, because a good marriage is based on the talent for friendship.

FRIEDRICH NIETZSCHE

I know that sex in marriage comes and goes. Sometimes we bring our fantasies along and sometimes not. Sometimes we act out childish petulance, distance the person we depend on most, go to sleep and dream of others. That is only human.

ERICA JONG

Often the difference between a successful marriage and a mediocre one consists of leaving about three or four things a day unsaid.

HARLAN MILLER

It is easier to be a lover than a husband, for the same reason that it is more difficult to show a ready wit all day long than to produce an occasional *bon mot*.

HONORÉ DE BALZAC

A simple enough pleasure, surely, to have breakfast alone with one's husband, but how seldom married people in the midst of life achieve it.

ANNE MORROW LINDBERGH

Every day that I'm with my wife [Kim Basinger], I want to read her mind. I'd make millions for that.

ALEC BALDWIN

Love is not being prettier or getting thinner; it's about how another human being feels when he's in your presence. Tell him you love him at least three times a day, and compliment him at least once.

ELLEN KREIDMAN

There is a lot to get used to in the first year of marriage. One wakes up in the morning and finds a pair of pigtails on the pillow that were not there before.

MARTIN LUTHER

Marriage has many pains but celibacy no pleasures.

SAMUEL JOHNSON

$\mathcal{I}$'ve said I loved myself too much to love anybody else, but that's no longer operative.

RUSH LIMBAUGH

$\mathcal{R}$ituals are important. Nowadays it's hip not to be married. I'm not interested in being hip.

JOHN LENNON

$\mathcal{I}$n cohabitation, people struggle to get society to see them as a couple. In marriage, it is difficult to get society to see them as individuals.

DR. CONSTANCE AHRONS

$\mathcal{K}$eep your eyes wide open before marriage, half shut afterwards.

BENJAMIN FRANKLIN

$\mathcal{A}$ married man forms married habits and becomes dependent on marriage just as a sailor becomes dependent on the sea.

GEORGE BERNARD SHAW

$\mathcal{M}$arriage isn't my thing. It scares me. The whole idea of "wife" is . . . *yech*. I guess I don't mind having a husband so much as I mind being a wife.

CYBILL SHEPHERD

$\mathcal{W}$hy does a woman work ten years to change a man's habits and then complain that he's not the man she married?

BARBRA STREISAND

For Better For Worse

Every marriage has its good days and its bad days. It has its ups and downs. Some have even compared marriage to a thrilling roller coaster. So let us toast the happy couple on what we are confident will be—for better or for worse— the ride of their lives.

*M*arriage involves big compromises all the time. International-level compromises. You're the U.S.A., he's the USSR, and you're talking nuclear warheads.

BETTE MIDLER

*T*rouble is part of your life, and if you don't share it, you don't give the person who loves you a chance to love you enough.

DINAH SHORE

*M*arriage is like life in this—that it is a field of battle, and not a bed of roses.

ROBERT LOUIS STEVENSON

All married couples should learn the art of battle as they should learn the art of making love. Good battle is objective and honest—never vicious or cruel. Good battle is healthy and constructive, and brings to a marriage the principle of equal partnership.

ANN LANDERS

The greatest happiness you can have is knowing that you do not necessarily require happiness.

WILLIAM SAROYAN

Two persons love in one another the future good which they aid one another to unfold.

MARGARET FULLER

[The secret of a lasting marriage is] mutual forbearance. We have each continued to believe that the other will do better tomorrow.

ROBERT MITCHUM

The critical period in matrimony is breakfast-time.

SIR ALAN PATRICK HERBERT

The last word is the most dangerous of infernal machines, and the husband and wife should no more fight to get it than they would struggle for the possession of a lighted bombshell.

DOUGLAS JERROLD

A married couple that plays cards together is just a fight that hasn't started yet.

GEORGE BURNS

The great secret of successful marriage is to treat all disasters as incidents and none of the incidents as disasters.

HAROLD NICHOLSON

Whenever a husband and wife begin to discuss their marriage, they are giving evidence at an inquest.

H. L. MENCKEN

Many waters cannot quench love, neither can the floods drown it.

KING SOLOMON

Well, all men are unfaithful anyway.

JACQUELINE KENNEDY ONASSIS

Once a woman has forgiven her man, she must not reheat his sins for breakfast.

MARLENE DIETRICH

Every six months we have a disaster. But I just get into gear and take care of business.

DR. LAURA SCHLESSINGER

It is a matter of life and death for married people to interrupt each other's stories; for if they did not, they would burst.

LOGAN PEARSALL SMITH

The happiness of married life depends upon making small sacrifices with readiness and cheerfulness.

JOHN SELDEN

A wife encourages her husband's egoism in order to exercise her own.

RUSSELL GREEN

They really don't know that there are going to be days when he's obnoxious or she's so tired she can't deal with him, or the fact that she may make more money than he does. The church tells them marriages are made in heaven, but so are thunder and lightning.

MICHAEL ALBANO,
President, American Academy of Matrimonial Lawyers

Happy, thrice happy and more, are they whom an unbroken bond unites and whose love shall know no sundering quarrels so long as they shall live.

HORACE

More than half of 72 couples reported declining satisfaction with their relationships during the two years after their first child was born, while only 20% said their marriage improved after starting a family.

CAROLYN PAPE COWAN AND PHILLIP COWAN,
Psychologists

Marriage is a book of which the first chapter is written in poetry and the remaining chapters in prose.

BEVERLY NICHOLS

For Richer For Poorer

*May your purse be full and
may you be rich with joy and
happiness, and when clouds gather,
may a rainbow be certain to
follow each rain.*

If thee marries for money, thee surely will earn it.

EZRA BOWEN

I don't believe it ever occurred to my husband to question my working, even when I earned less than the cost of our household help.

ESTHER PETERSON

I've had an exciting life; I married for love and got a little money along with it.

ROSE FITZGERALD KENNEDY

If you don't learn to laugh at trouble, you won't have anything to laugh at when you're old.

ED HOWE

You are looking for a rich husband. At your age, I looked for hardship, danger, horror and death, that I might feel the life in me more intensely. I did not let the fear of death govern my life; and my reward was, I had my life. You are going to let the fear of poverty govern your life and your reward will be that you will eat, but you will not live.

GEORGE BERNARD SHAW

Last year I handed my father a hundred dollars and said, "Buy something that will make your life easier." He went out and bought a present for my mother.

RITA RUDNER

The trick is to make sure you don't die waiting for prosperity to come.

LEE IACOCCA

Marriage halves our griefs, doubles our joys, and quadruples our expenses.

ENGLISH PROVERB

Prince Charming may be telling you that you have no equal, but that won't do much good when you've got kids and a mortgage—and he has a beer gut and a wandering eye.

ANN RICHARDS

Marriage, like money, is still with us; and, like money, progressively devalued.

ROBERT GRAVES

Show me one couple unhappy merely on account of their limited circumstances, and I will show you ten who are wretched from other causes.

SAMUEL TAYLOR COLERIDGE

If both the husband and wife are successful by their own standards, and not necessarily the materialistic standards of the world, the marriage can be a fulfilling one.

SHEPHARD G. ARONSON

In Sickness and In Health

May you always have each other, in sickness and in health. May you always be a healing presence and treat each other tenderly, care for each other thoughtfully, and live for each other throughout your lives.

Do you know that it frightens and unmans me to know that you are sick. Your health is the continent, the solid land on which I build all my happiness and hope. When you are sick, I am like the inhabitants of countries visited by Earthquake. They lose all faith in the eternal order and fixedness of things. Your sickness is my Earthquake.

JAMES A. GARFIELD

It's odd that you can get so anesthetized by your own pain or your own problem that you don't quite fully share the hell of someone close to you.

LADY BIRD JOHNSON

Comfort me with apples, for I am sick of love.

KING SOLOMON

Night after night George held me weeping in his arms while I tried to explain my feelings. I almost wonder why he didn't leave me. I knew it was wrong, but couldn't seem to pull out of it.

BARBARA BUSH,
Remembering her period of depression

No man knows what the wife of his bosom is— what a ministering angel she is, until he has gone with her through the fiery trials of this world.

WASHINGTON IRVING

I don't think the significance of getting married hit us until then. It's a totally new feeling to lean on someone, and I never thought I'd be able to do it, even with [James] Carville.

MARY MATALIN,
After suffering two miscarriages

There you are you see, quite simply, if you cannot have your dear husband for a comfort and a delight, for a breadwinner and a crosspatch, for a sofa, a chair or a hotwater bottle, one can use him as a Cross to be borne.

STEVIE SMITH

Who loves the rain and loves his home, and looks on life with quiet eyes, him will I follow through the storm and at his hearth-fire keep me warm.

FRANCES SHAW

My husband thinks that health food is anything he eats before the expiration date.

RITA RUDNER

What greater thing is there for two human souls than to feel that they are joined for life—to strengthen each other in all labor, to rest on each other in all sorrow, to minister to each other in all pain, to be one with each other in silent, unspeakable memories at the moment of the last parting.

GEORGE ELIOT

Illness has to be one of the tests of a marriage. That's why they put it in the marriage vows. Everyone sorta glides over it, but it's important. For the first time, you are caught naked with your pretenses down. . . . You are vulnerable and you are dependent. Neither of you married to have the other partner "take care of you."

ERMA BOMBECK

To Love and To Cherish

Today, on this happy day, it is natural to dote on one another, to hold each other precious. So let us toast the bride and groom, and ask them to remember the feeling of this day. In all your married days that follow, may you remember the love that brought you together today, and may you cherish one another with the same concern, affection, and devotion that brought this day to pass.

To love is to place our happiness in the happiness of another.

GOTTFRIED WILHELM VON LEIBNITZ

Marriage is three parts love and seven parts forgiveness of sins.

LANGDON MITCHELL

The particular charm of marriage is the duologue, the permanent conversation between two people who talk over everything and everyone.

CYRIL CONNOLLY

The way to a man's heart is through his stomach.

FANNY FERN

Positive Reinforcement is hugging your husband when he does a load of laundry. Negative Reinforcement is telling him he used too much detergent.

Dr. Joyce Brothers

The heart that loves is always young.

Greek proverb

Cherish all your happy moments: they make a fine cushion for old age.

Booth Tarkington

Whether you are loved or not depends more on others than on anything *you* do.

Erica Jong

$\mathcal{A}$ happy marriage perhaps represents the ideal of human relationship—a setting in which each partner, while acknowledging the need of the other, feels free to be what he or she by nature is: a relationship in which instinct as well as intellect can find expression; in which giving and taking are equal; in which each accepts the other, and *I* confronts *Thou*.

Anthony Storr

$\mathcal{T}$here isn't a wife in the world who has not taken the exact measure of her husband, weighed him and settled him in her own mind, and knows him as well as if she had ordered him after designs and specifications of her own.

Charles Dudley Warner

*E*ach coming together of man and wife, even if they have been mated for many years, should be a fresh adventure; each winning should necessitate a fresh wooing.

MARIE CARMICHAEL STOPES

[*I* credit our long-lasting marriage to] our mutual faith in God and in each other.

JUNE CASH

[*I* credit our long-lasting marriage to] commitment, and separate bathrooms.

JOHNNY CASH

If I could not be myself, I would like to be Mrs. Choate's second husband.

JOSEPH HODGES CHOATE

Of course, I do have a slight advantage over the rest of you. It helps in a pinch to be able to remind your bride that you gave up a throne for her.

DUKE OF WINDSOR,
Formerly King Edward VIII

The man who falls in love with a strong and independent woman and then tries to tame her . . . is not loving but conquering; a common romantic plot ever since *The Taming of the Shrew*. The woman who is obsessed by the question "How can I change him?" is not centered in her own life but trying to control his; a plot that's common when women marry their lives instead of leading them.

GLORIA STEINEM

She is but half a wife that is not, nor is capable of being, a friend.

WILLIAM PENN

Teacher, tender comrade, wife,
A fellow-farer true through life.

ROBERT LOUIS STEVENSON

There is nothing nobler or more admirable than when two people who see eye to eye keep house as man and wife, confounding their enemies and delighting their friends.

HOMER

Now join your hands, and with your hands your hearts.

WILLIAM SHAKESPEARE,
King Henry the Sixth, Part III

One of the oldest human needs is having someone to wonder where you are when you don't
come home at night.

Margaret Mead

Man and woman are two locked caskets, of which
each contains the key to the other.

Isak Dinesen

Shang ya!
I want to be your friend
For ever and ever without break or decay.
When the hills are all flat
And the rivers are all dry,
When it lightens and thunders in winter,
When it rains and snows in summer,
When Heaven and Earth mingle—
Not till then will I part from you.

ANONYMOUS,
Oath of Friendship,
CHINA, 1ST CENTURY B.C.

*L*ove is a flame which burns in heaven, and
whose soft reflections radiate to us. Two worlds
are opened, two lives given to it. It is by love that
we double our being; it is by love that we
approach God.

AIMEE MARTIN

❧ 48 ❧

Till Death Us Do Part

Till death us do part reminds us of the strength of the commitment that marriage represents. So let us offer a toast to the happy couple:

May you both live long and prosperous lives. May you remain steadfast in your commitment to one another, and may you know the enduring joy and contentment that comes only from spending a loving lifetime together.

Marriage: A legal or religious ceremony by which two persons of the opposite sex solemnly agree to harass and spy on each other for ninety-nine years, or until death do them join.

ELBERT HUBBARD

Seven of those days were pretty good. The eighth day was the bad one.

DENNIS HOPPER,
Reflecting on his eight-day marriage to Michelle Phillips

Even now, we have laryngitis from screaming at each other: the dirty little secret of a durable marriage. I'll never divorce him—how can I, he's a divorce lawyer—but I may just shoot him. This is the way two people know they're mated.

ERICA JONG

Grandchildren don't make a man feel old; it's the knowledge that he's married to a grandmother.

G. NORMAN COLLIE

The very fact that we make such a to-do over golden weddings indicates our amazement at human endurance. The celebration is more in the nature of a reward for stamina.

ILKA CHASE

An old man in love is like a flower in winter.

PORTUGUESE PROVERB

Marriage is a lot like the army: everyone complains, but you'd be surprised at the large number that re-enlist.

JAMES GARNER

Young love is a flame; very pretty, often very hot and fierce, but still only light and flickering. The love of the older and disciplined heart is as coals, deep-burning, unquenchable.

HENRY WARD BEECHER

Both marriage and death ought to be welcome: the one promises happiness, doubtless the other assures it.

MARK TWAIN

There is no place like a bed for confidential disclosures between friends. Man and wife, they say, there open the very bottom of their souls to each other; and some old couples often lie and chat over old times till nearly morning.

HERMAN MELVILLE

The happy married man dies in good stile at home, surrounded by his weeping wife and children. The old bachelor don't die at all—he sort of rots away, like a pollywog's tail.

ARTEMUS WARD

It gets worse every day. Thirty-five years ago I told Sam to come home and I'd fix him lunch. He's been coming home for lunch every day for thirty-five years.

FRANCES GOLDWYN

A long-term marriage has to move beyond chemistry to compatibility, to friendship, to companionship. It is certainly not that passion disappears, but that it is conjoined with other ways of love.

MADELEINE L'ENGLE

When marrying, one should ask oneself this question: Do you believe that you will be able to converse well with this woman into your old age?

FRIEDRICH NIETZSCHE

However old a conjugal union, it still garners some sweetness. Winter has some cloudless days, and under the snow a few flowers still bloom.

MADAME DE STAËL

Forty years. One man!

MATILDA CUOMO,
On her 40th anniversary, in disbelief

My mother buried three husbands, and two of them were just napping.

RITA RUDNER

The sum which two married people owe to one another defies calculation. It is an infinite debt, which can only be discharged through all eternity.

JOHANN WOLFGANG VON GOETHE

A happy marriage is a long conversation which always seems too short.

ANDRÉ MAUROIS

Heaven will be no heaven to me if I do not meet my wife there.

ANDREW JACKSON